BY KIRSTEN W. LARSON

AMICUS HIGH INTEREST · AMICUS INK

Amicus High Interest and Amicus Ink are imprints of Amicus
P.O. Box 1329, Mankato, MN 56002
www.amicuspublishing.us

Library of Congress Cataloging-in-Publication Data
Larson, Kirsten W., author.
Super powers in nature / by Kirsten W. Larson.
pages cm. – (Freaky nature)
"Amicus High Interest is an imprint of Amicus."
Summary: "This photo-illustrated book for elementary readers describes animals with amazing speed, strength, and senses. Explains how these adaptations benefit them as defenses against predators or as ways to find and capture prey"– Provided by publisher.
Audience: K to grade 3.
Includes bibliographical references and index.
ISBN 978-1-60753-781-6 (library binding) –
ISBN 978-1-60753-880-6 (ebook)
ISBN 978-1-68152-032-2 (paperback)
1. Animals–Adaptation–Juvenile literature. 2. Animal behavior–Juvenile literature. 3. Adaptation (Biology)–Juvenile literature. 4. Senses and sensation–Juvenile literature. I. Title.
QH546.L37 2016
591.4–dc23

2014036514

Editor: Wendy Dieker
Series Designer: Kathleen Petelinsek
Book Designer: Heather Dreisbach
Photo Researcher: Derek Brown

Photo Credits: Alamy / Andrew Harrington 19; Alamy / blickwinkel 10; Alamy / Dave Watts 9; Alamy / imageBROKER 15; Alamy / Louise Heusinkveld 5; Alamy / The Science Picture Company 6; Corbis / Momatiuk - Eastcott 12; David C. Blackburn, Ph.D. 27; Shutterstock / David Evison 21; Shutterstock / Ewan Chesser 25; Shutterstock / Four Oaks 16; Wikimedia Commons / Dr. Matjaž Kuntner / Creative Commons 2.5 22; Jolanta Dąbrowska / Alamy cover

Printed in Malaysia

HC 10 9 8 7 6 5 4 3 2 1
PB 10 9 8 7 6 5 4 3 2 1

Table of Contents

What Are Super Powers?

Comic book heroes have “magical” powers. Powers like super strength help them beat bad guys. Pow!

Like superheroes, animals have **adaptations** that help them survive. Some have super senses. They hear or smell things people cannot. Others have extra senses. Some have super strength or speed. Other animals use super tools like webs or claws.

Tigers have super tools like long, sharp teeth and claws that are great for hunting.

Even the largest water bear is barely big enough to be seen without a microscope.

Where do water bears live?

Then, there are some really amazing animals. Almost nothing destroys them. Meet the tiny water bear. Starve this tiny creature for 10 years. Dunk it in boiling water. Dry it out like a raisin. Send it to outer space. The water bear survives everything by **hibernating**. It seems dead. But it is alive. Talk about super powerful!

Water bears live almost anywhere. They live in water. They live in the ground under your feet. They also live in ice.

Super Senses

The platypus dives into the river. Splash! Flaps of skin cover its eyes and ears. It even plugs its nose. How does it know when tasty shrimp shoots by? Just like Spider-Man, the platypus has a sixth sense. When shrimp move, their muscles make electrical signals. Sensors on the platypus's bill detect the signals. The animal snaps up its snack. Smack!

The platypus doesn't need its eyes to find a tasty meal.

The aye-aye uses its long finger to tap the bark and then to scoop bugs out.

What other animals use sound to map their world?

At night, the aye-aye looks for food using super hearing. It taps a tree trunk with its long middle finger. The taps echo off bugs moving beneath the bark. The aye-aye hears the echoes. Then it knows dinner waits inside. The animal chews through the bark with rabbit-like teeth. It scoops out the food. Slurp.

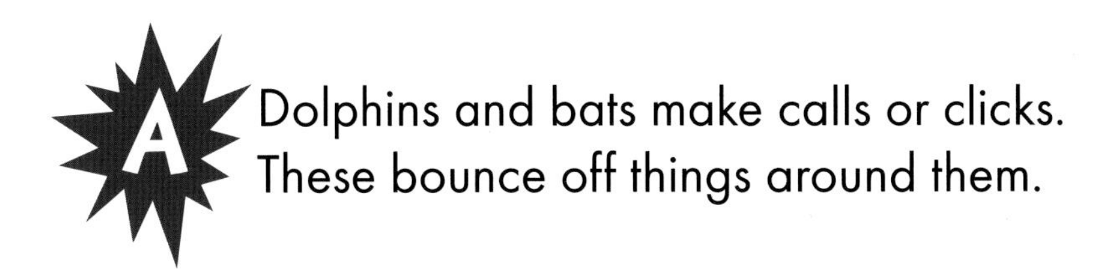

Dolphins and bats make calls or clicks. These bounce off things around them.

The wandering albatross spends days gliding above ocean waves. Using its super sense of smell, it sniffs squid from 3 miles (4.8 km) away. The bird can smell the squid even underwater. The bird flies toward its lunch. It dives straight down into the ocean. Gulp! It eats the squid.

The wandering albatross uses its strong sense of smell to find food.

Super Abilities

Lost a leg? For the Mexican axolotl, that is no problem. It has an amazing super **ability**. It can regrow the lost limb! First, the animal's wound heals. Then its new body part grows. This takes about a month. The new limb works as well as the first. The animal is just like new.

Can other animals can regrow body parts?

Some axolotls are even able to regrow parts of their brain and spine!

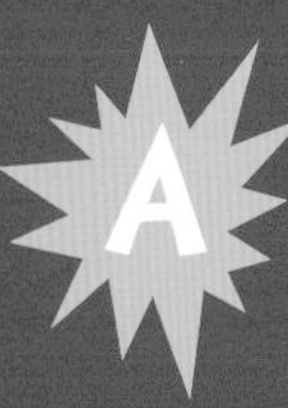

Yes! Sea stars can regrow legs too. And some lizards can regrow a lost tail.

Dung beetles roll poop to their homes. They lay eggs on it.

What makes the beetles so strong?

Dung beetles have Hulk-like strength. The thumb-sized animal weighs about as much as two grains of rice. But it can pull 1.2 ounces (34 g). That's like a person lifting five African elephants all at once. It is the strongest animal for its size. Dung beetles need strength to battle each other. Males lock horns. They push each other from underground tunnels.

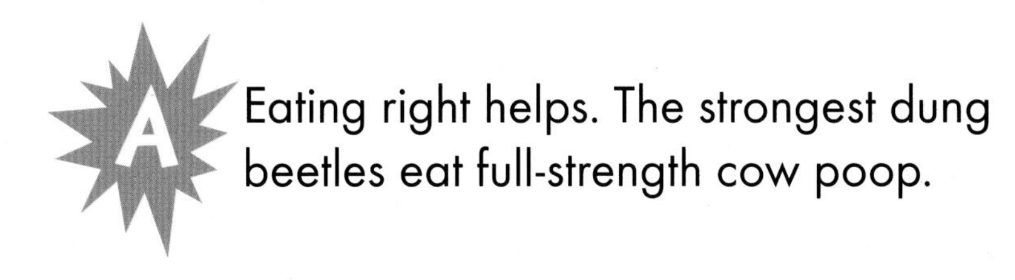

Eating right helps. The strongest dung beetles eat full-strength cow poop.

Superman flies faster than a speeding bullet. Cheetahs can't run that fast, but they are super fast too. They run at highway speeds. But scientists recently found something faster. In one second, a seed-sized mite races 322 times its body length. That is like a person running twice as fast as an airplane.

Cheetahs are able to run more than twice as fast as the fastest human.

This mimic octopus can twist itself into many shapes to hide from enemies.

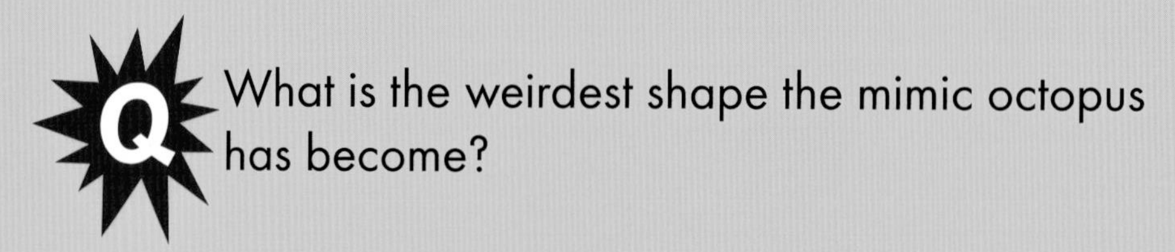

What is the weirdest shape the mimic octopus has become?

Now you see it. Now you don't. Some superheroes are masters of disguise. Octopuses are too. They change color and texture to blend in. The mimic octopus takes this one step further. It shifts its shape. Now it looks like a different animal. Is that a sea snake? No. It is the octopus. Look out for the lionfish! No, that's the octopus too.

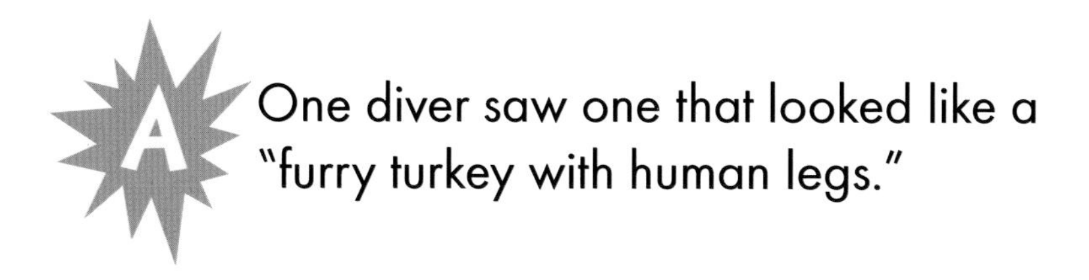

One diver saw one that looked like a "furry turkey with human legs."

Super Tools

Spider-Man's super strong webs are a lot like real spider silk. Spiders use special **glands** to spin many types of silk. Some stretch like rubber. Others are as strong as steel. The Darwin's bark spider spins webs across wide rivers. Now that is strong silk!

Some webs are so strong they can even catch birds and bats.

The honey badger's super tough skin is excellent protection.

What other **defenses** does the badger have?

A honey badger's skin is as tough as Iron Man's armor. The badger is called the most fearless animal in the world. It hunts snakes and bee **larvae**. The badger's skin resists bee stings. It stops knives. Nothing scares this badger. It will even bite a lion. Talk about tough armor!

It has long claws. Watch out! And even more amazing, snake venom does not kill it. Wow!

When the superhero Wolverine gets mad, claw-like blades shoot from his hands. When the hairy frog gets scared, it grows claws too. First, bones in its back feet snap apart. The bones poke through the skin. Look out! These claws are dangerous. African hunters use long knives to hunt the frogs. They do not want to get scratched.

Tiny bones poke out of the frog's toes when it is frightened.

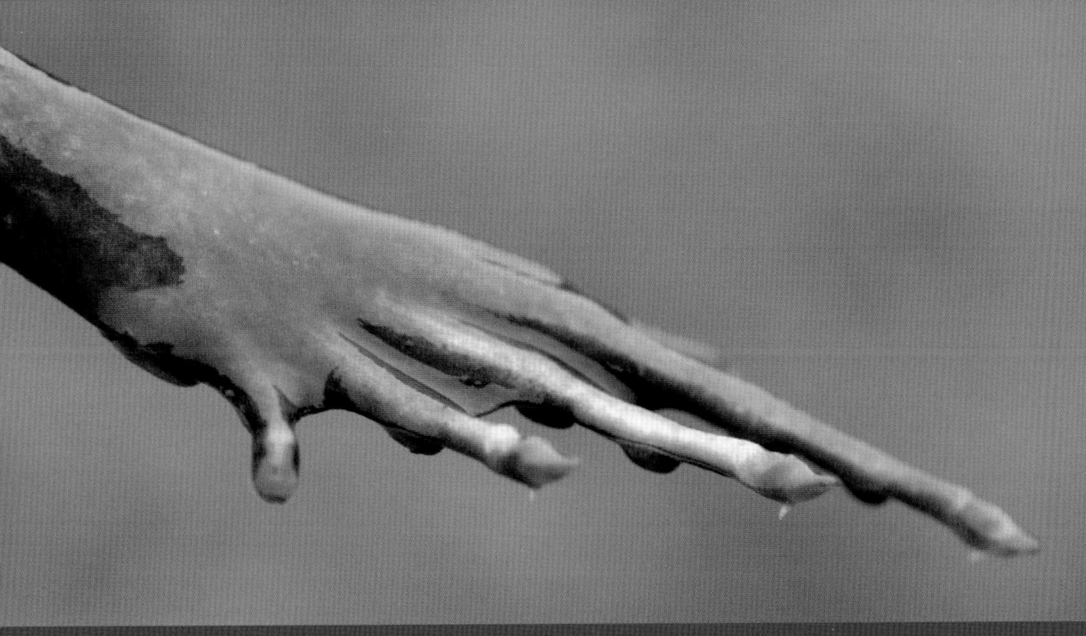

Bats use sound and their super senses to find food and find their way in the dark.

Nature's Superheroes

Like superheroes, animals use their abilities to fight bad guys. But in the animal world, the bad guys are **predators**. Without their powers, the animals could become lunch. Munch!

Animals' powers help in other ways too. Sometimes they help find or trap food. Look around. There are super powers everywhere in nature!

Glossary

ability The power to do something.

adaptations Changes in living things that make them better able to survive in their environment.

defense Something that protects an animal from predators.

glands Small organs in an animal's body that make or release something important, such as sweat or saliva.

hibernating To become inactive and sleepy for a long period of time, especially during winter.

larvae An insect in its second stage of life, when it looks like a worm.

predators Animals that hunt and eat other animals.

Read More

Heos, Bridget. *Stronger Than Steel: Spider DNA and the Quest for Better Bulletproof Vests, Sutures, and Parachute Rope.* New York: Houghton Mifflin Harcourt, 2013.

Montgomery, Heather L. *Wild Discoveries: Wacky New Animals.* New York: Scholastic Inc., 2013.

Wood, Alix. *Weird Animals in the Wild.* New York: Windmill Books, 2014.

Websites

Ranger Rick Animals—National Wildlife Federation
www.nwf.org/kids/ranger-rick/animals.aspx

San Diego Zoo Bytes
animals.sandiegozoo.org/

PBS Kids | Wild Kratts Creaturepedia
pbskids.org/wildkratts/creaturepedia/

Index

About the Author

Kirsten W. Larson used to work with rocket scientists at NASA. Now she writes about science for children. She's written more than a dozen magazine articles and two books for children. Her favorite part of writing this book was studying up on superheroes. Wonder Woman was her childhood favorite.